Your I

MIMI NOVIC

Aspiring Hope
Publishing

Copyright © Mimi Novic 2018

All rights reserved. No part of this publication may be reproduced, stored in a retrieval system, or transmitted in any form or by any means, electronic, mechanical, photocopy, recording or otherwise, without prior written permission of the copyright owner. Nor can it be circulated in any form of binding or cover other than that in which it is published and without similar condition including this condition being imposed on a subsequent purchaser.

British Library Cataloguing Publication Data. A catalogue record for this book is available from the British Library.

Book design by Metech Multimedia Ltd.

Graphic Artist Carmine Lella.

Special thanks to Katia Lella Wellbeing & Life Coach for her wonderful effort, valuable insight and inspirational words.

ISBN 978-1-9999120-1-7

Published by Aspiring Hope Publishing

About the Author

Mimi Novic is one of today's most highly respected self-awareness teachers and inspirational life coaches in the fields of self-development and spiritual growth.

Through Mimi's various ground-breaking healing techniques, many have learnt to gain wellness in mind, body and spirit as well as developing positive thinking techniques to gain greater freedom to achieve a more balanced and peaceful life.

Through her work as an alternative medical practitioner, therapist, voiceover artist, author and motivational speaker, she encourages everyone, from whatever walk of life they may be from, to embark upon the journey of self-discovery, in order to heal their lives.

Mimi teaches seminars and workshops in alternative medicine and self-awareness, as well as complementary and holistic therapies, working around the world in clinics, retreats and on a one to one basis.

Her thought provoking writings are also available as a series of meditation albums, which beautifully harmonise her inspirations with soul enlightening music, that awaken the heart and bring peace and serenity back into our lives.
An expert in her field, Mimi continues to help people find their life's purpose, through her continuing motivational work.

Introduction

Go with the flow
Sing with excitement
Let your cares fall away
Create your own music
Stay positive
Celebrate in your uniqueness
Make a difference in the world.

You are extraordinary
You are unique
You are a heart and soul that contains a whole universe
Now is the time to start to believe in your power within.

Take this little book of inspiration by the hand and let it be a daily reminder of all things that are bright, wonderful, positive and that all things are possible if you trust your heart.
Have an amazing life!

Dedication

Eternally grateful to one of the brightest stars I know and whose guiding light made me see the light within myself, my mama.

And to you my beloved guide, whose hand is forever in mine, I wait in the moonlight until we meet again.

Contents

Chapter 1   Don't Compare Yourself to Others
Chapter 2   Feeling Lonely
Chapter 3   Feeling Afraid
Chapter 4   Feeling Sad
Chapter 5   Feeling Angry
Chapter 6   Feeling Unsure
Chapter 7   Feeling Lost
Chapter 8   Don't Give Up
Chapter 9   Have Hope
Chapter 10   Be Happy
Chapter 11   Believe in Your Dreams
Chapter 12   Believe in Yourself
Chapter 13   Be Positive
Chapter 14   Follow Your Heart
Chapter 15   Believe in Love

Chapter 1
Don't Compare Yourself to Others

By comparing
ourselves to others
we lose precious time
which could be spent
accomplishing our
own achievements

Don't try to be like
everyone else
Always be yourself
The world needs
your talent

Just because
someone looks
similar to you
Doesn't mean they
are the same as you
Everyone has their
special gift

Everyone likes
different things and
different people
Find what and who
makes you happy

Everyone is beautiful
Because they are
unique

Chapter 2
Feeling Lonely

We all have an angel
that is sent to look
after us when we are
born

You are part of a
huge universe
Take a deep breath,
put your hand on
your heart and feel it
beating
You are here for a
reason

Every day the sun rises and shows us that with each new sunrise we can start again

Your heart is your
best friend
Trust what it tells
you

Say a prayer, let it go
and let it fly on
angels wings to
God's door

Chapter 3
Feeling Afraid

Don't let your fear
make you feel weak
Accept everything in
life as a lesson and
you will learn from
every experience and
gain strength from it

You may sometimes
feel the darkness
around you
Take it as an
opportunity to shine

God always sees you
and He will show
you the way through
your heart

We can overcome
everything that
doesn't bring us
peace by adapting
ourselves
Each difficulty is an
opportunity to be
better than before

Don't hide from your fears
Let your fears hide from you

Chapter 4
Feeling Sad

Nobody likes to feel
the pain of sadness
But we need to walk
through it so that we
may know what
makes us happy

We all have days
when we can't stop
the tears from falling
Stay calm and
peaceful as your tears
are preparing you to
see your dreams
more clearly

Don't run away from your feelings
As they are the keys that unlock your strength

Your smile has the
power to chase away
the clouds and the
shadows and make
the darkness in your
day disappear

Do something wonderful for yourself today
Feel the music inside and dance
There are so many reasons to be happy if you look in the right place

Chapter 5
Feeling Angry

We are never really lost
We just sometimes forget to read the signs that life is showing us

No victory will come
to you in life without
understanding
yourself
Every question you
have, you already
have the answer
Look deep within

Sometimes all we
need to do is to open
the door to our heart
and see what's inside

Remain calm
Everything that is
happening right now
is bringing you closer
to knowing yourself

Not every wrong turn means that you are lost
It might be the only way to find the right path

Chapter 6
Feeling Unsure

Don't let anyone
make you so angry
that it destroys
everything good
inside of you
As you will have to
live with your
actions for the rest of
your life

You can never control other people
You can only control yourself
Be the one who makes things better as you will reap the rewards

Be careful with the words you speak
They are able to either lift or break hearts

Your anger always
shows your weakness
to another person
Don't allow them to
use it against you
Your power is your
ability to stay calm

Have discipline with
your emotions
Your reactions
determine the
outcome of every
situation

Chapter 7
Feeling Lost

The secret is to always trust your heart even in the most difficult moments
Take your time and be patient
Everything comes to us at the right time

There are many ways
to look at things that
happen to you
You can either take it
as a lesson and
become stronger or
you can allow it to
make you weaker
The choice is yours

Every life has its
twists and turns
Be like the wind
adjust yourself and
go with the flow

Unless you try you
will never win
You can never lose
when you're doing
your best

When you cant
decide what the right
thing to do is
Always choose what
gives peace to your
heart

Chapter 8
Don't Give Up

Just as the rain needs to come and give life for nature to flourish You must allow your tears to fall, washing away your sadness and making way for new opportunities

When you look with
your heart
You can see the
magical in
everything

For every storm that comes your way it's always a chance to clear away all that you no longer need The future always look brighter when the clouds of doubt pass

For every struggle
For every tear
For every sadness
For every smile
For every happiness
There's something to
be learnt that gives
us the strength to
continue our dreams

We are the only ones
who can decide
whether we want to
achieve success
Remain focused on
your goal

Chapter 9
Have Hope

The most beautiful place that exists is within you

Don't ever forget
there's only one of
you in the whole
world that can make
the difference that
only you can

Everyday hope
whispers to you
"Don't give up"
There is always
something wonderful
that is waiting to
happen

Nothing can begin
unless we make a
choice to start
You are here for a
reason and your life
has a purpose

Hope is the silent
prayer that every
heart hears
Let it take your hand
and be your guide

Chapter 10
Be Happy

Be with those that celebrate your presence in their life and make you feel liberated and alive
Be with those who make your heart full of beautiful moments

Start each day with gratitude
You've been given another chance today

It's only as
complicated as we
make it
Choose simplicity,
it's the fastest way to
feeling peaceful

Sometimes we have
to keep learning the
same lesson
Until we decide we
want to make a
change

Whatever we see on
the outside of us
is a reflection of what
we see on the inside
of ourselves
Change your
thoughts and your
world changes

Chapter 11
Believe in Your Dreams

We have the power
within us
We just forget
sometimes
Don't waste your
precious life energy
on anything that
doesn't bring you
closer to your soul
purpose

The biggest mountains we have to climb are those within us

Never doubt yourself
This is the secret key
to every opportunity

Do something beautiful for yourself today

Don't chase the
shadows of your past
Or you will miss the
light of today

Chapter 12
Believe in Yourself

Sometimes the only way to find the answers is not to travel far away but to venture deeper within ourselves

You don't need anyone's permission to be yourself

To accept yourself is to know yourself Knowing who you really are changes everything

Be the energy you want to attract

When you remember
who you are
You will be free

Chapter 13
Be Positive

There is one thing we must never forget to do while we are here
To live and experience an amazingly wonderful life in all its joy and beauty

Have courage
There is nothing
more powerful than
your light to banish
all the shadows of
the world

It's not about it
being easy
It's about it being
worth it

The greatest courage comes from walking away from every situation that doesn't bring harmony to your life

What we think, we attract
When we change our attitude we change our life

Chapter 14
Follow Your Heart

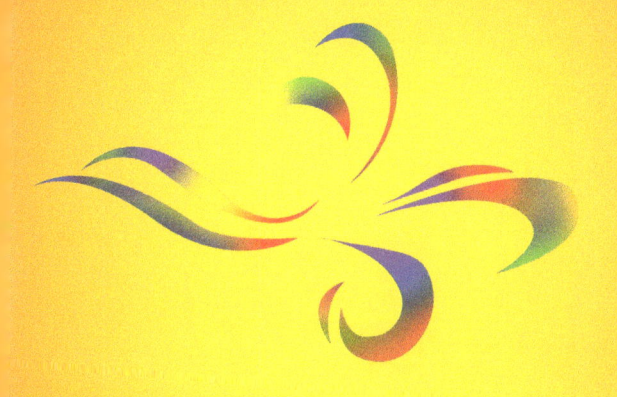

The real treasures are
found by following
the map of our heart

We all have our own lives and stories that we live in and only our footsteps can travel along the road that is meant for us

Start walking
towards where your
soul feels free

There are no
coincidences
It's guidance
To remind us of our
path

You see all those stars
in the sky?
They're shining for
you to find your way

Chapter 15
Believe in Love

No matter how
different we all look
We all share the same
wishes of the heart
That make us want
to feel loved and
accepted

We are only ever one
step and one breath
away from changing
our life
Keep what you love
Let go of everything
else

If you ever feel the need to pretend or hide your true self, then you are with the wrong people Surround yourself with those that accept you for who you are

Sometimes all it takes to make a difference in someone's life is to hold their hand and to let them feel they are loved

We all speak to each other in a language beyond words
Only those that listen with their hearts can hear what we say